W9-BZW-031

CHESAPEAKE BAY WALK

by **David Owen Bell**

illustrated by

Jennifer Heyd Wharton

Tidewater Publishers
Centreville, Maryland

Text copyright © 1998 by David Owen Bell
Illustrations copyright © 1998 by Jennifer Heyd Wharton
Printed on recycled paper in Hong Kong

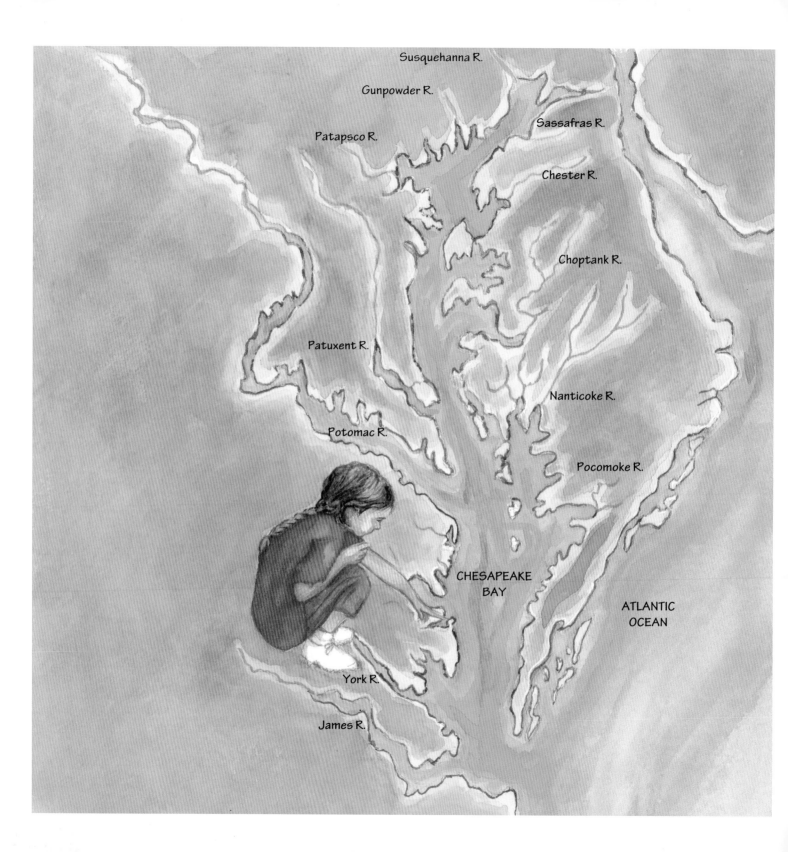

Susquehanna R.

Gunpowder R.

Sassafras R.

Patapsco R.

Chester R.

Choptank R.

Patuxent R.

Nanticoke R.

Potomac R.

Pocomoke R.

CHESAPEAKE
BAY

ATLANTIC
OCEAN

York R.

James R.

THE CHESAPEAKE BAY
IS AN AMAZING PLACE!

It has many different habitats, which are places for plants and animals to live. Beaches, marshes, and shallow waters are homes to all sorts of life. The shoreline of the Bay, and of the many rivers and creeks that feed it, is a great place to find living things. Let's go for a Chesapeake Bay walk!

SHORELINE

Sandy beaches, marshes, and mudflats are different kinds of natural shoreline habitats. The piers and jetties that people build also give plants and animals places to live.

ONCE HUNTED FOR THEIR FEATHERS

Great blue herons look for food in shallow waters along the shore. They catch fish, crabs, worms, and insects with their bills. Adult herons are four feet tall and their spread-out wings measure six feet from tip to tip, but they weigh less than seven pounds. How much do you weigh?

THEY TURN "BALD" AT AGE FIVE

More bald eagles live around the Chesapeake Bay than almost anywhere else in the United States. Young eagles are brown all over. By age five, their head feathers turn white. Eagles live in treetop nests along the shore. They use their claws, called talons, to catch fish and small animals.

BEACH

Sandy beaches are good places to find shells, driftwood, and other treasures that have washed ashore. During the day, beach hoppers and fleas are found in the sand or under rows of dried weeds at the high-tide line. Sometimes you can see them jumping around near the water. How high can you jump?

Also look for bird feathers and footprints. Try to find a shell with algae or a barnacle growing on it. How many different kinds of shells can you find?

OLDER THAN THE DINOSAURS

In late spring, adult horseshoe crabs come from deep water to lay their eggs on sandy beaches along the southern half of the Bay. Many of the eggs are eaten by hungry birds. The eggs that hatch are washed back into the water by the tide.

Horseshoe crabs were already ancient history when dinosaurs walked the earth. Pieces of their thin brown shells can be found on Chesapeake beaches.

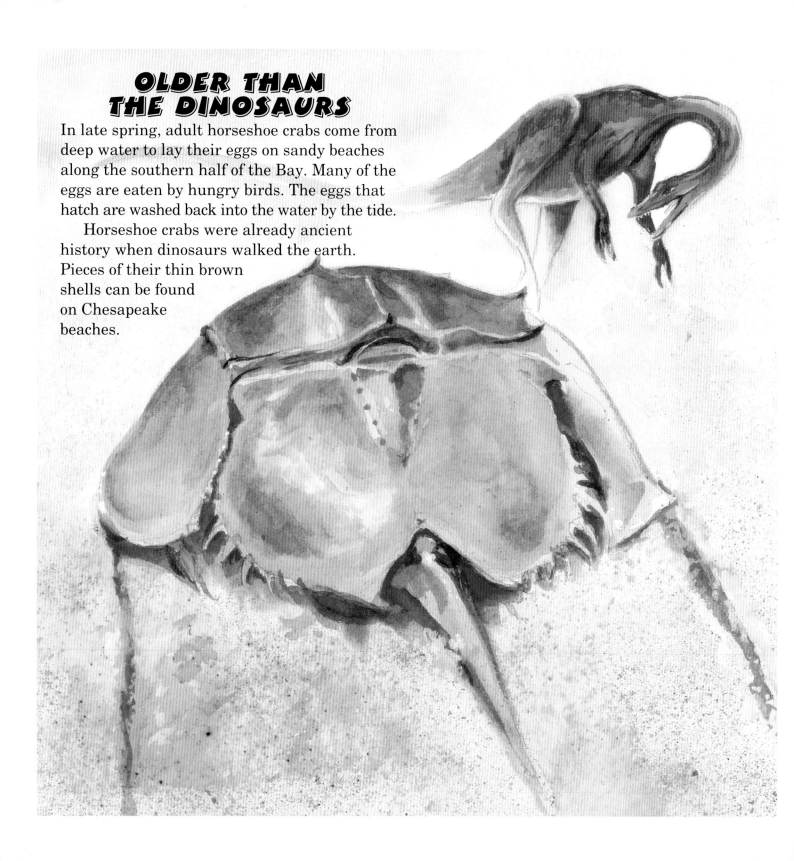

SHELL SHEDDERS

Like other crabs and shrimp, blue crabs molt, or shed their shells, as they grow. Cast-off crab shells can be found washed up on beaches. The heat of the sun turns them red. Live crabs are found all around the Bay, from deepwater mud in the winter to shallow water around piers in the summer.

LIVING WATER PUMPS

An oyster has two shells, one flat and the other rounded. Oyster shells are rough on the outside and smooth on the inside. Oysters live on the bottom of the Chesapeake Bay and some of its rivers.

As oysters grow, so do their shells. Oysters eat tiny plants that drift in the water. To get enough food, oysters pump up to fifty gallons of water through their bodies every day. (A gallon is the size of a large milk container. Can you imagine fifty of them?)

MARSH

Marshes are filled with grasses and weeds that provide shelter and food for many animals. Squirts, barnacles, and sponges attach to eelgrass. Snails, slugs, shrimp, and fish move among the plants in search of food. Frogs, snakes, birds, and muskrats also make the marsh their home.

THEY MAKE THEIR OWN FOOD

Bay weeds and grasses grow in shallow water and along the shore. Being plants, they use water, nutrients, carbon dioxide, and the sun's energy to make their own food. Nutrients, like vitamins, help living things grow. These plants attract animals from the air (like ducks), from the land (like muskrats), and from the water (like snails, shrimp, crabs, and fish) who make the plants their food.

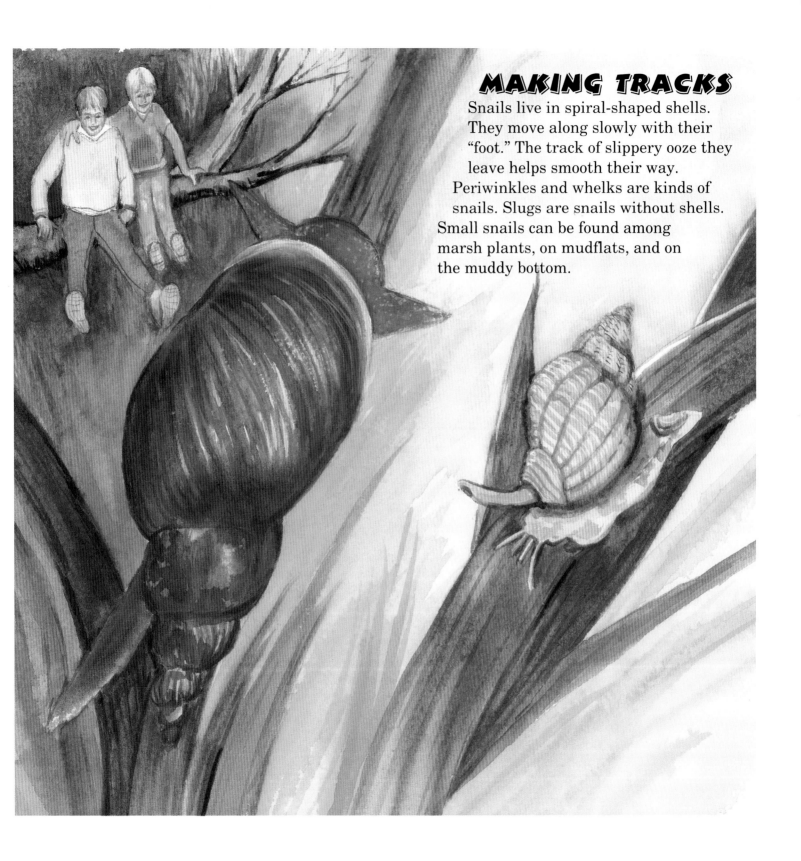

MAKING TRACKS

Snails live in spiral-shaped shells. They move along slowly with their "foot." The track of slippery ooze they leave helps smooth their way. Periwinkles and whelks are kinds of snails. Slugs are snails without shells. Small snails can be found among marsh plants, on mudflats, and on the muddy bottom.

Mudflat

Mudflats are home to fiddler crabs, hermit crabs, worms, snails, and bugs. Small plants that are attached to rocks or shells also grow here. Take off your shoes for a cool, squishy walk in the mud.

BULLIES OF THE BAY

Hermit crabs live along the southern half of the Chesapeake Bay. These crabs don't grow shells. To protect their soft bodies, they have to find shells in which to live. Sometimes they find empty shells, and sometimes they take them from other animals. They need to find bigger and bigger shells as they grow.

THEY COME WITH THEIR OWN STRAW

Clams live in the mud. To eat, they open their shells and take in water through a tube, filtering or straining it for whatever small bits of food they can catch.

BORING IS EXCITING

There are many different kinds of worms living all around the Bay. Some live in tubes that they build, and others bore or burrow through the mud. Worms are food for fish, birds, and crabs. The best place to find them is a mudflat at low tide.

PIER

The green stuff you often see growing on rocks in the water is algae. Algae and other plants, barnacles, mussels, and sponges also attach to wooden pilings that hold up the piers in harbors around the Chesapeake Bay. Shrimp, worms, and bugs come in search of food.

THEY MAKE THE BAY'S STRONGEST GLUE

Once barnacles stick to something, they stay for life. You can find hard-shelled barnacles glued to boat bottoms, pilings, mussel shells, bottles, and rocks. Barnacles catch tiny bits of passing food with their legs.

NOT FOR THE BATHTUB

Chesapeake Bay sponges are tiny animals living inside a red, purple, or green "sponge." They grow on rocks and pilings in the water and can sometimes be seen at low tide.

SHALLOWS

In the shallow waters along the Chesapeake Bay and its rivers and creeks you might find fish, crabs, shrimp, and jellyfish. The water in the Chesapeake Bay is brackish—a mixture of freshwater and saltwater. The freshwater comes from falling rain, flowing rivers, and melting snow. The saltwater comes from the Atlantic Ocean.

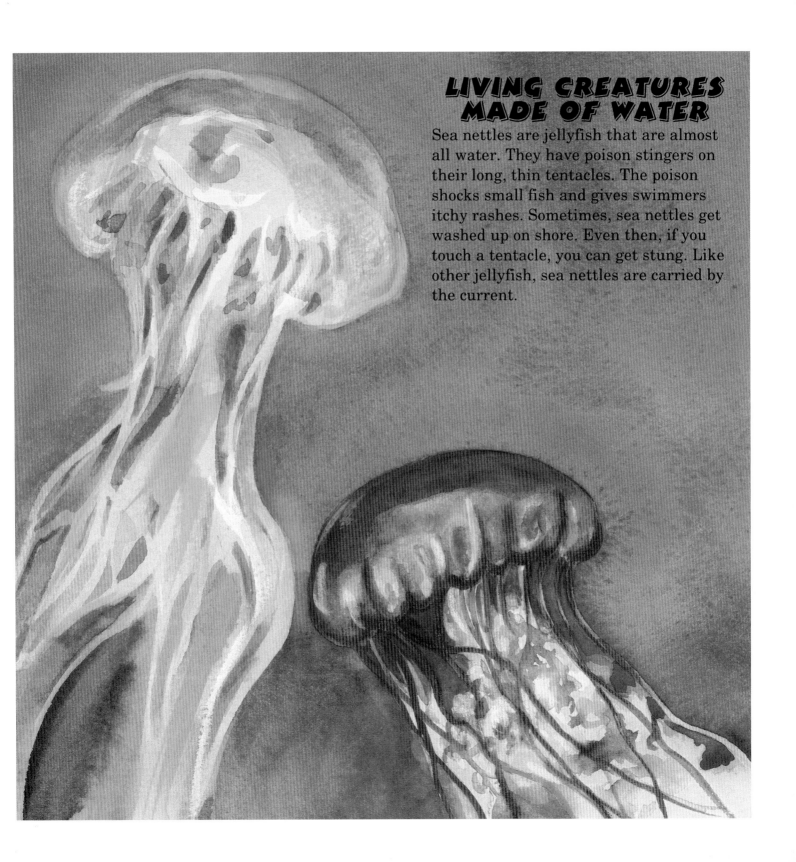

LIVING CREATURES MADE OF WATER

Sea nettles are jellyfish that are almost all water. They have poison stingers on their long, thin tentacles. The poison shocks small fish and gives swimmers itchy rashes. Sometimes, sea nettles get washed up on shore. Even then, if you touch a tentacle, you can get stung. Like other jellyfish, sea nettles are carried by the current.

DRIFTING NIGHT LIGHTS

Comb jellies are drifters, too, eating whatever tiny bits of food happen to be nearby. These jellyfish don't sting. Because they are clear, they are hard to see in the water—but at night, they give off a pale green glow.

LOOK AT THEIR STRIPES

Striped killifish are found in shallow waters during the warmer months. In the winter, they move to deeper water. The young have vertical (up and down) stripes, as do the males (boys). Female (girl) striped killifish have horizontal (side to side) stripes.

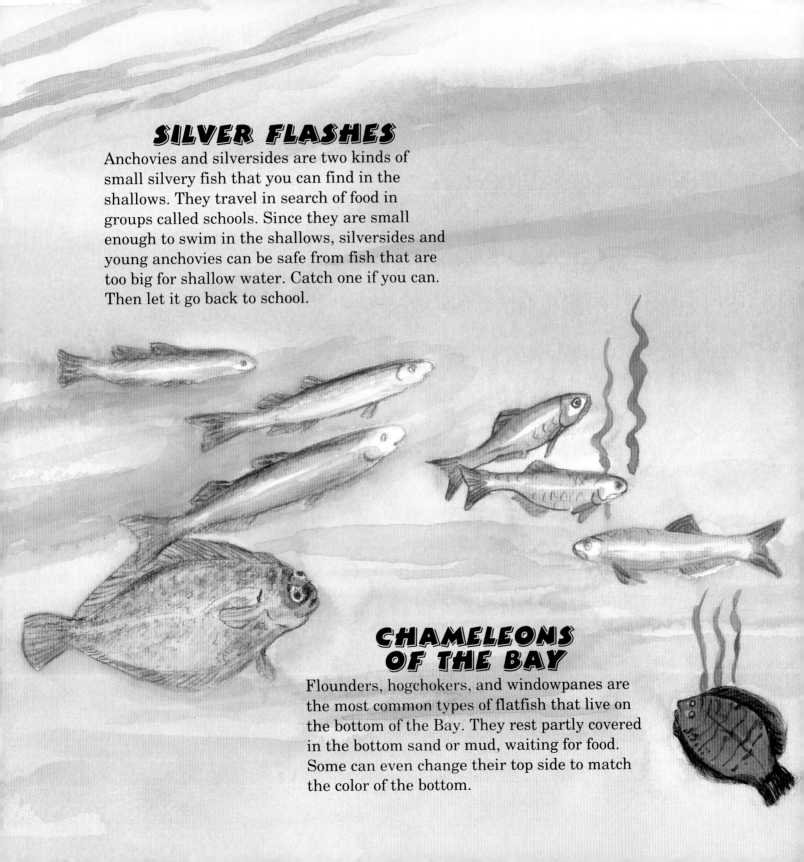

SILVER FLASHES

Anchovies and silversides are two kinds of small silvery fish that you can find in the shallows. They travel in search of food in groups called schools. Since they are small enough to swim in the shallows, silversides and young anchovies can be safe from fish that are too big for shallow water. Catch one if you can. Then let it go back to school.

CHAMELEONS OF THE BAY

Flounders, hogchokers, and windowpanes are the most common types of flatfish that live on the bottom of the Bay. They rest partly covered in the bottom sand or mud, waiting for food. Some can even change their top side to match the color of the bottom.

THE CHESAPEAKE BAY

The plants and animals in Chesapeake Bay habitats need each other, like links need other links to make a chain. The Chesapeake Bay food chain starts with tiny plants called algae. There are many different kinds of algae.

You can see some algae attached to rocks, pilings, and other solid objects. Other algae drift freely in the water. These single drifting plants are so small, you need a microscope to see them.

Algae in the water are eaten by small drifting animals. Another name for drifters is plankton.

Animal plankton include jellyfish, comb jellies, and baby fish, crabs, and oysters. Plankton are eaten by clams, oysters, and fish such as anchovies that can strain or filter the water for food.

Anchovies, silversides, and other small fish are eaten by bigger fish like white perch, which are eaten by even bigger fish like bluefish. Fish are caught and eaten by birds like great blue heron, eagles, and gulls.

Crabs and catfish eat clams and mussels. They also eat dead fish and bits of plants. Tiny bacteria—even smaller than algae—eat dead plants and animals and turn them into soil. Soil has nutrients that algae and other plants can use.

People eat crabs, clams, oysters, and fish. What do you eat that might have come from the Bay?

FOOD CHAIN

CHESAPEAKE SEASONS

In March, Canada geese fly home to Canada as osprey return to the Bay from South America. As the days get longer and warmer in the spring, fish, birds, and insects hatch. Spring rain and melting snow carry soil rich in nutrients to the Chesapeake Bay. Nutrients help algae and other plants grow. These plants are food for the tiny fish that have hatched.

By early summer, flowers are in full bloom and young birds are leaving their nests. Fish called Atlantic menhaden come from the ocean to the Chesapeake Bay to feed on plankton—the tiny animals that drift with the currents of the Bay.

In early fall, Canada geese begin to arrive for the winter. Osprey head back to South America. Monarch butterflies pass through on their yearly journey south.

As the days get shorter, turtles, frogs, and crabs bury themselves for the winter. By midwinter, eagles and owls start laying their eggs. Soon, spring will come, and the cycle of life will begin again.

How many of these things
have you found on your
Chesapeake Bay walks?

algae	horseshoe crab
anchovy	killifish
barnacle	muskrat
beach hopper	mussel
blue crab	osprey
clam	oyster
comb jelly	sea nettle
duck	shrimp
eagle	slug
eelgrass	snail
fiddler crab	snake
flatfish	sponge
frog	squirt
goose	turtle
great blue heron	worm
hermit crab	

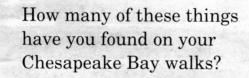